MACMILLAN READERS

STARTER LEVEL

C. J. MOORE

Alissa

macmillan education

Macmillan Readers is a series of engaging narrative texts designed to stimulate learners while enhancing their language skills, building literacy and boosting reading confidence. Through captivating stories and fascinating cultural themes, learners will explore a diversity of scenarios that foster vocabulary expansion, comprehension skills and a lifelong love of reading.

The right reader at every stage
Tailored to each learner's stage of language proficiency, our six levels feature text adapted to match the skill level. With controlled vocabulary and grammar, learners can read freely and immerse themselves in the story. When more challenging words are introduced, either the text will provide sufficient context to aid understanding or a full explanation will be provided in the Glossary.

Readers for all, anywhere, anytime
Macmillan Readers are perfect for shared, guided and independent reading. Whether in traditional print, immersive audio or the convenient eBook, Macmillan Readers are equally effective for in-class activities, paired discussions or solo reading at home or on the move.

Reading for pleasure, knowledge and well-being
Regular reading and reading for pleasure:

- increases reading confidence, benefiting all literacy skills, not just reading.
- reinforces and enriches vocabulary, providing a variety of contexts.
- expands general knowledge.
- supports concentration, inner reflection and well-being.

Macmillan Readers will inspire a love for reading in English while nurturing essential language skills. Unlock new worlds, expand horizons and embark on an adventure in English!

(NOTE: While the content of Macmillan Readers is evaluated for age suitability, we kindly remind parents and teachers that they are ultimately responsible for determining whether a particular book is appropriate for their child or student.)

Alissa is reading. Her father calls to her. 'Alissa! Alissa!'

Alissa runs to the door. There is a car outside the house. Her father is talking to a fat man.

'This is Alissa. She reads all day,' her father says. The two men laugh.

'Alissa,' her father says. 'My friend has work for you in the city. There isn't any work here in the village. You must go with him.'

The fat man smiles at Alissa.

'How old are you?' he asks.

'I'm twelve,' she says.

The fat man laughs again. Alissa doesn't like him. She doesn't want to go with this man. She wants to go to school in the village. She likes school. She likes reading.

'Your mother is packing your things. You must go to the city,' her father says.

The fat man gives some money to Alissa's father. Alissa's father is pleased and happy. Alissa is angry and afraid.

Alissa does not want to go with this man. But she must obey her father.

Alissa and the fat man arrive in the city. They drive to a house. A thin man comes to the door. The two men talk.

'Here is your room,' the thin man says to Alissa. He points to a door under the steps.

Alissa goes into the room. The room is small and dark. It is her new home.

The next morning, the thin man takes Alissa into the house.

'This is Alissa,' the man says to his wife. 'She likes reading.' They laugh.

Suddenly the woman shouts at Alissa. 'You aren't going to read here,' she shouts. 'You're going to cook and clean and wash.'

Alissa works fifteen hours a day. The woman shouts at her every day. Alissa is very unhappy. She cries every night.

One day, the thin man says to Alissa, 'Pack your things. You must go. My wife doesn't like you.'

The thin man takes her to a clothes shop in the city. The shop owner is a large woman. She gives the man some money. He goes away. He doesn't say goodbye to Alissa.

Alissa works with five other girls. They work in a small, dark room.

The girls work all day. They make clothes. They work twelve hours a day. At midday, they eat lunch. After lunch, they rest for ten minutes. At night, they sleep on the floor.

Each month, the shop owner gives the girls a little money. Alissa buys a book with her money. She reads the book after lunch.

The shop owner is surprised. The other girls can't read.

'Can you write? Can you count?' the shop owner asks.

'Yes, I can,' Alissa says.

'Come,' the shop owner says. 'You are going to work in the shop.'

Alissa likes working in the shop. She serves the customers. The customers are rich ladies. They buy expensive dresses.

One of the customers is a tall and pretty lady. She always smiles at Alissa. She gives Alissa small presents.

One day, the tall lady leaves her purse in the shop. Alissa runs out into the street. She runs after the lady.

'Here is your purse,' Alissa says. The lady smiles. She takes some money from the purse.

'Thank you,' she says to Alissa. 'You are an honest girl. Take this money.'

'No, no,' says Alissa. 'I don't want your money.'

She runs back to the shop. The shop owner shouts at her.

'Don't leave the shop again!' she shouts. 'I pay you a lot of money. I pay you to work. I don't pay you to run out into the street.'

Alissa is angry.

'You don't pay me a lot of money,' she shouts. 'I'm a slave here.'

'You're an ungrateful girl,' the large woman says. 'You have a bed and food and money. Do you want more?'

'Yes, I do,' Alissa says. She is crying now.

'Wait,' a quiet voice says. The tall lady is standing at the door.

'Alissa isn't ungrateful,' the tall lady says. 'She is an honest girl.'

The tall lady speaks to Alissa.

'Aren't you happy here?' she asks. 'What do you want?'

Alissa says, 'I want to go to school.'

The tall lady turns to the shop owner. 'Alissa will live in my house,' she says. 'She won't work. She will go to school.'

'You must pay me,' the shop owner says.

'No,' the tall lady says, 'Alissa isn't a slave.'

'Pack your things, Alissa,' she says. 'We will go home now.'

Alissa goes with the tall lady. She is going to a new home. She is going to be happy.

Macmillan Education Limited
4 Crinan Street
London N1 9XW

Companies and representatives throughout the world

Macmillan Readers Starter Alissa
ISBN: 978-1-035-15116-5
Macmillan Readers Starter Alissa with eBook and Resources
ISBN: 978-1-035-15119-6

First published 1989
This edition published 2024

Illustrated by Kay Dixie
Cover photograph by Getty/Vikram Raghuvanshi

Printed and bound in Brazil
2025
3